Tawan Perry

SOPHOMORE
SUCCESS

Your step-by-step guide to achieving every
goal and having a great time in
your second year of college

COPYRIGHT NOTICE

PUBLISHER'S NOTE

Due to the dynamic nature of the Internet, any web addresses or links contained in this book may have changed since publication and may no longer be valid. This publication is designed to provide accurate and authoritative information in regard to the subject matter covered. It is sold with the understanding that the author and publisher are not engaged in rendering legal, accounting or other professional services. If you require legal advice or other expert assistance, you should seek the services of a competent professional.

TABLE OF CONTENTS

ACKNOWLEDGMENTS

Cynthia * You are truly a blessing. Your work is incredible, and I'm so glad you're on my team.

Ayman * Your artistry is a gift from above. Thanks for everything.

All My Sophomore Students * Thanks for all the hard work that you put in. Never forget that it all starts with you!

TO ALL SOPHOMORE STUDENTS

No one ever said that being a student is easy. As a former student myself, I completely understand the challenges that all students encounter, so I have written this book with you in mind.

This guide covers several important topics, such as selecting the right major the first time, becoming an "A" student your sophomore year, how to reconnect with faculty, staff and your peers, and how to find and take advantage of studying aboard, internship, and networking opportunities.

Whether you struggled with your first year or were a straight "A" student, this guide will help you to create an enriching collegiate experience your sophomore year and beyond.

Sophomore students will also discover:

- Resources to help you overcome the sophomore slump
- How to manage your money and avoid student debt
- Effortless ways to acquire meaningful experiences, such as service learning opportunities, internships, and study aboard
- How to choose a major that best reflects your values and passion

Thank you for your investment in this book and your trust in my expertise to help you make this a successful year.

Tawan Perry, M.Ed.
Get Connected. Stay Connected. Graduate.

INTRODUCTION

While many books focus on the first year of college, the sophomore student is often forgotten. Very similar to your first year of college, you will be challenged by both your academic and social experience, and both will impact and conflict with each other at times.

This book is divided into five chapters that cover a myriad of topics that relate directly to and affect your success during your sophomore year. Its purpose is to help you overcome the challenges that are unique to sophomore students.

The sophomore year is one of the toughest years, but ironically, it is a year when you receive the least amount of support, unless you take the initiative to make it happen. Part, if not all, of your success ultimately depends on your efforts this year.

As a predecessor on this journey, I have thought of everything to make your current year more successful. So take the time to read every page, as all of the information is relevant to your success. Use this book as a blueprint to help you experience a meaningful, memorable, and fun sophomore year, for finding success in your second year of college…and beyond!

PART 1

I've Survived My First Year, Now What?

Sophomore Considerations

Congratulations! You made it to your sophomore year. However, the journey ahead is far from over. Your sophomore year is truly the year for trying new things and seeing how they work. If it doesn't work out, you learn from it and move forward.

You will succeed as long as you remember that all experiments require effort. The people who succeed are not those who are just smart, strong or talented. People who succeed are those who are willing to try, and when they fail they get back up.

As a sophomore you will have many decisions to make: What major do you plan to declare? Will you live on or off campus? Will you study aboard your junior year? Decisions! Decisions! Decisions!

Before you get overwhelmed, let's take a step back and formulate a game plan. There are two goals here: first, to give you a blueprint for returning on campus; and second, for you to figure out what is most important to you. That is, what do you want to get out of this year? The following is your blueprint for returning to campus.

If you are attending a 4-year institution, once you have returned to campus, here is your Action Plan:

1. **Put forth a vision and set goals. It's a new year and that means new goals.** Success

always begins with a vision and stated goals. By setting goals, you will remain focused on what it is you need to do. Ask yourself daily, "Am I moving closer to my goal, or am I regressing?"

2. If you have transferred from another institution and have sophomore standing (usually 30 or more credits), **attend orientation**. Although you are not a first year student, if your institution offers an **orientation** program, be sure to attend it. At most institutions, orientation programs are offered either in the summer or during the first week of school.

Orientation is designed to enable you to have a smooth transition into the institution. During orientation, you will have the opportunity to learn about academic and social expectations, meet other students, learn about the university's services and resources, become acquainted with the campus, and meet campus administrators. As a sophomore, you may know how to be a college student, but you will not know about the campus culture and environment.

3. **Go to the Cashier/Bursar Office**. Be sure that your finances are in order. Pay all of your bills or be sure to secure a payment plan. Also, keep all of your receipts. Be sure to **renew your student identification card. This may require you getting a new sticker or having the card reactivated to reflect that your balances are paid. Either way, make sure that your card has full function before school starts.**

4. **Secure housing**. Be sure to secure your housing. This is something you want to take care of once you make the decision to attend the institution. If you are planning to live on campus, you can contact your **Housing or Residence Life** office. If you do not plan to live on campus, this office usually has a relationship with landlords off campus.

No matter where you choose to live, you will need to fill out another housing application. When filling out a housing application, you will need to pay the application fee and put down a security deposit, present a form of identification (driver's license or student identification card), and provide proof of income (if you plan to live off campus). Your proof of income is usually in the form of your financial aid award letter.

5. **Get your meal plan**. Decide if you want to get a meal plan. If you live on campus, some institutions require a minimum meal plan. Before you purchase and activate your meal plan, you should ask if it is required. If you don't ask, the institution may charge you for the meal plan without you ever formally signing up for it. In any case, every institution is different.

Additionally, the meal plans differ at each institution. Choose a meal plan that best accommodates your eating habits. After all, you can upgrade your meal plan anytime. A good resource for this type of information is my book, *College Sense: What College and High School Advisors Don't Tell You about College.*

6. **Parking. As a sophomore you will more than likely have the privilege of having a**

car on campus. Before you bring your car on campus, contact the **Parking Services Office** (sometimes the same as the campus police office) and get a temporary pass. Also, know the parking policies ahead of time. This may save your car from being towed.

7. **Schedule an appointment with your Academic Advisor**. Your academic advisor can help you create a good schedule. Be sure to keep all paperwork from the previous year to ensure that there is no mix-up. Ask them to assist you with class registration, if necessary.

8. **Purchase your books**. Find out what textbooks you need before classes start by emailing the professors ahead of time. This will save you from very long lines in the bookstore. Also, you may want to consider renting your text books from websites like www.chegg.com or www.campusbookrentals.com. However, be sure you know when the books are due. Don't make the mistake of having to return your books the same week you are taking finals.

9. **Refamiliarize yourself with various offices**. By refamiliarizing yourself with various offices, you will become connected with other services, other students, and other staff members. Also, it's a good idea to reacquaint yourself, as some offices may have new faces.

10. **Locate your classes before the first day**. This will save you time and embarrassment the first day of class. This is particularly important if you are a sophomore transfer student.

11. **Be excited**. You are one step closer to completing your degree and fulfilling your dreams!

In summary, if you are attending a community college, here is your **Second Year Action Plan:**

1. Establish new goals.
2. Attend orientation (if applicable).

3. Go to the Cashier/Bursar Office (pay bills, renew student ID).
4. Secure housing (on/off campus).
5. Get your meal plan.
6. Go to Parking Services (if applicable).
7. Schedule/meet with academic advisor (to schedule/register for classes, as needed).
8. Purchase your books.
9. Familiarize yourself with some of the offices and/or centers.
10. Locate your classes.
11. Be excited!

Note: If you go to the school's website, student handbook or catalogue, you may find an action plan for that specific school. In addition, some schools have a central location where you can go to get most of these things taken care of. However, you will have to seek some things on your own.

Now that you have your game plan for the first week of school, let's talk about what you want to get out of this year. Some items are listed below. Order them from 1-10 (one being the least important).

This year I would like to:

___Declare my major
___Join a student organization
___Join a Greek organization
___Become an officer of my student organization
___Get out of my room more
___Meet more people
___Improve my GPA
___Draft or update my resume
___Get an internship relevant to my declared
 major
___Volunteer in the community
___Raise money for a cause
___Spend more time with family and friends
___Study aboard
___Obtain an internship
___Become a resident assistant
___Mentor first year students
___Find a mentor
___Get into less trouble

___Live off campus with friends
___Make more friends
___Experience off campus living
___Figure out my purpose for being in school
___Start an organization
___Get a part-time job
___Identify service learning opportunities
___Take the GRE, LSAT, or other test
___Buy a car

What were your top five choices?

1.
2.
3.
4.
5.

If none of these items appeals to you, what would you like to do?

If I could accomplish only one thing this year, it would be _____.

As you can see, the possibilities for your second year in college are limitless! Just find something you are passionate about and make it happen.

Reconnecting to the Campus Community

During your first year, you may have utilized some of the resources to your advantage. However, this year you will need to become reacquainted with these resources, and in some cases reach out to new resources.

When students think of college resources, they usually think about people who work in the offices. While that certainly makes sense, one of the most overlooked resources in college is your peer group. A wealth of experience and expertise exists at your fingertips both in the classroom and on campus. As one of my **mentors** once told me, "At a university you should never be afraid to ask for help." So be open to assistance, because it's not what you know, it's *who* you know.

If you plan to continue living on campus, get to know the following individuals:

Resident Assistants

Resident Assistants may also be referred to as Resident Advisor, Fellow Community Leader, or other similar name. If this is your first time living on campus, the resident assistant is the seasoned student leader who lives on your floor in the residence hall and is there to assist you. The **RA** usually knows things about the school, and if they don't, they can point you in the right direction. At most institutions they are your most important resource, and usually among the first people you meet.

Residence Director

Residence Directors are also referred to as the Community Director, Hall Director, or Area Coordinator. Similar to high school principals, they manage all operations of the residence halls. Residence directors are live-in educators professionally trained to mediate and resolve crises. Additionally, they supervise the RAs. They are some of the most informed and knowledgeable professionals at the institution, because they often collaborate with other campus offices and departments. If you didn't have a good experience with your residence director last year, it's time to develop a positive relationship during your sophomore year.

Professors

Because professors issue your grades, their opinions matters considerably. Although some professors may seem unreachable because they have limited office hours (specific times they set aside to meet with students), it would be wise to try to meet with them outside of class at least once during the semester. If the professor or teaching assistant can place a name with a face, that can make the difference in a grade (especially if the grade is borderline). Visiting professors during office hours can also help clear up confusion about upcoming tests, assignments, and the course **syllabus.**

Administrative Assistants

Get to know the administrative assistants of different offices, perhaps the most important people in the office. They are the gatekeepers of the person you wish to contact and decide when you can see that person. You can be either a familiar face or just another student who comes to the office, so it pays to get to know them personally. They are usually knowledgeable and have information others in the office won't know.

Tutors

I cannot say enough about these students who can lead you to the promised land of "graduation." Tutors are helpful in two ways. First, they assist with understanding course objectives, with homework assignments, quiz and test review. And second, being high achievers themselves, they can help you find scholarships and other financial aid. At many institutions, tutors are honor students in the good graces with the offices awarding the scholarships. They can also provide advice on what courses to take.

Special Interest / Multicultural / Office Staff Members

If you are from an underrepresented group, these offices often provide an extra layer of support. They also are very knowledgeable with regard to financial aid, special opportunities, and social networks especially designed for underrepresented groups.

Other important contacts include the following support staff and administrators: Academic Advisors, Transfer Advisors, Peer Mentors, Financial Aid Staff, Department Chair, Vice-President of Student Affairs or Vice-Chancellor, Deans, and Student Government Association members.

If you attend a community college, get to know these individuals:

- Transfer / Academic Advisor
- Faculty Member / Instructor
- Administrative Assistants
- Peer Mentors / Leaders
- Student Support Office Personnel
- Multicultural / Special Interest Staff Members
- Financial Aid Administrators

The aforementioned list of people you should know is by no means comprehensive. Similar to your first year, your second year is not meant to be a solo journey. In order to build and continue your success, you must be willing to allow others to assist you. Besides, everyone at an institution of higher education contributes to your success: housekeepers, professors, clerical staff, librarians, the cooks. Just as it takes a village to raise a child, similarly, it takes a higher education institute to graduate a student.

PART 2

Avoiding the Sophomore Academic Slump

Improving Grades as a Sophomore

Your first job in college is to be a student. As a sophomore you will be given more opportunities and, as a result, you will make more decisions. You may be approached with the proposition to make more money, take on more leadership roles, and get more co-curricular experiences. While all of this is fine, your most important job this year is to make sure that you get a better sense of what it will take for you to get your degree.

The only way to ensure that this happens is to focus your activities on learning. For some, this is the part of college that is extremely difficult. Make no mistake; your sophomore year can still be enjoyable. However, it is also a time to focus on learning and establishing the skills necessary for you to begin a career.

Whether you had a great academic year as a first year student, or it didn't go quite the way you wanted it to doesn't matter anymore; because this is a new year, and with a new year come new challenges and opportunities. If you take the time to fully develop relationships with your professors and instructors and utilize your resources, it is impossible to fail.

The following tips will assist you in your academic journey through your second year.

Tip #1: Be Flexible.

Although you do not always have control over what comes your way, you always have control over how you respond. For that matter, do not expect things to always go your way. For this reason alone, there are few things in life that are life and death, but life and death.

Tip #2: Know Your Place.

If you are having difficulty in reading, you should find a comfortable location and choose a regular reading place and time. In all my years of college, I never knew a student who had the same regular place; you just have to find what works for you. For some students, their place is the library; for others, their room is their best choice.

Tip #3: Experiment.

By now, you have probably completed many of your general education courses, and this may be just the time for you to begin experimenting with what your ultimate major will be. I cannot stress this enough. If you have electives, use this as an opportunity to explore different classes. During my sophomore year, I experimented with speech classes, computer science, and a business course. While I ultimately declared a different major, I was able to make a more informed decision about what I was passionate about and what I wasn't passionate about. The lesson here: Use your electives as a way to engage your interest.

Tip #4: Get Started.

Get started with your homework, in spite of whether or not you like it. Once you start, you may find it easier to continue. I have found this especially true for writing papers. Every person has days when he or she cannot seem to get started doing something, but the key is that you start. When it comes to things like writing papers, motivation can come and go. The hardest part is just getting started. The process of writing papers for college is not that different from the process of writing you used for high school. You can always go back and change things before the given deadline.

Tip#5: Anticipate Exam Questions.

This is very important for many exams, especially for essay exams. When writing down possible questions, write out the answers prior to the exam and memorize the main points. By doing this, when you get to similar questions on the exam, you will not be easily rattled. Consequently, you will not take up a lot of time trying to write an answer.

Tip#6: Reorganize Your Notes.

If your handwriting is as bad as mine, rewrite your notes within a day in order to organize and expand the information. If you wait too long, you may not remember the details later. Moreover, rewriting your notes is an excellent study tool to help you remember the information.

Tip #7: Steer the Course.

Make sure you are taking classes that will keep you on course. That means meeting with your advisor and making sure you are closing in on graduation requirements. There is nothing worse than feeling like you've wasted your time.

Tip #8: Be Selective in Your Reading.

If you want to be quicker with your reading, keep in mind that only some material is worth studying and the rest is just worth skimming. Begin with an overview and get a bigger picture and context of the book. Or read by skimming through the table of contents, introduction and conclusion, key chapters, and the first and last paragraphs of each chapter. This will give you a sense of the overall theme of the reading and its main points.

Tip #9: Focus On and Mark Key Points.

As you read, focus on key points and mark them. When you go back, it can serve as a quick reference. This can be done by using asterisks, highlighting sentences, and numbering the sequence of events.

Tip #10: Know Your Learning Style.

There are usually three types of learners: visual, auditory, and tactile. If you are having trouble figuring out your learning style, or if you just don't know where to begin, go to the career or counseling center and take an assessment. Kolb's Learning Style Inventory is one such assessment inventory. Also, remember that study techniques are very subjective. What might work for your friend might not work for you, and vice versa. If you take an assessment test your first semester of college, you will benefit greatly from the results.

Tip #11: Study with a Friend.

Enlist a friend and study the subject together. However, by all means, study with someone who can help you with the subject. Sometimes we hinder ourselves more by adding more distractions.

Tip #12: Balance.

Make sure you LOL, GTC, and have FUN. Balance is key. School is an educational and social experience, not a vacation. Believe me, when you graduate from school, you'll know just how good you had it.

Tip #13: Do the Easy Part First.

Sometimes if you do the easy part first, it may give you motivation to continue. I found this to be helpful with math and science. Doing the easy part first gives you momentum, and once you get momentum, it's much easier to stay focused on what must be done.

Tip #14: Form Study Groups.

If you are struggling in a particular subject, ask a group of classmates to join you in forming a study group. Study groups are great because you can quiz each other, divide sections, and become experts in specific sections.

Tip #15: Utilize Tutorial Services.

Someone once told me that if I did not go to see the tutor for help, the tutor still got paid. In most cases, if no one visits, the tutor socializes with others or works on his/her own homework. This is a fact. I had many tutors in college because of all my difficulties in math and science. Although I still had to work hard, the tutors helped to make the concepts easier to understand. One thing is certain, whenever I made the point to keep regular appointments with a tutor, I never failed a test and I never had to repeat a class. The lesson here is clear: When in college, do not be afraid to ask for help!

Declaring the Right Major

So you are nearing the end of your sophomore year and you still don't know what you want to declare. Don't feel bad, it's perfectly natural. In fact, the sad truth is that some people spend the majority of their adult lives working a job for a living that they hate and, as a result, never feel good about going to work each day.

Find the thing that makes you happy (no matter how it sounds to others), because your life depends on it. It is not about the money, and it is not about what others think. Instead, it's about how you want to live your life every day. So don't feel pressured to make a hasty decision about selecting a career or a major.

The best thing you can do is to continue experimenting as you figure out what you want to do. Life is about continuing to learn and figuring out our purpose, and there is no way for you to decide all of this in one year. However, if you know what you don't want to do by your second year of college, you are making progress.

You will find that although what you do today may not seem relevant, with time things start to come together. It doesn't matter if it seems as though everyone else knows what they plan to do with their life. Believe me; they don't.

College is the time for you to discover who you are, what you enjoy doing, what you are good at doing, and what you want to be. We are all a work in progress. Choosing a career is not a race, so take your time and enjoy exploring your options. Moreover, don't worry; the money will come eventually.

<u>Things to Consider</u>

- What did I like about the course?
- What didn't I like about the course?
- Can I see myself working in this field?
- What is the best use of my time, a class or an internship?
- Can I do both?
- What's the best thing about this major?
- Will this take me off course from my goal?
- What is my dream and what am I going to do to get there?

One of the hardest things to figure out in college is deciding on the right career choice for you. Consider the following helpful tips.

Tip #1: When Changing Majors, Do Not Feel Discouraged.

You are not alone! There will always be thousands of students who change their major in college. It's more important to find out what interests you now, than declaring a major only to regret it later. The best thing about having the option to change your major several times while still in college is that you get to take the time to discover who you are and where you want to be. Sure, this process of discovery may be time consuming, but even more time consuming is going to work every day, hating what you do, and finally realizing that the job you have is not the job for you.

Tip #2: Take an Inventory.

When exploring potential majors, you should spend time getting to know yourself, your abilities, and your motivations. The first task I suggest is to visit your Career Services office and take a career assessment as soon as possible. This will help you better understand what types of jobs or careers appeal to you, your strengths and weaknesses. This service usually is underutilized, but it can be very beneficial.

Additionally, ask yourself the following:

- What are my strengths?
- What are my weaknesses?
- What would I do for free? What do I really enjoy?
- What skills do I have?
- What were my best subjects in high school?
- What extracurricular activities did I participate in, in the past?
- What skills did I learn from part-time or summer jobs?
- What things do I value in life?
- What do I value in a job or career?
- What are some other resources to help me get more information about a major and/or a career?

Tip #3: Take a Variety of Classes.

Choosing a college major is a process just like selecting a school to attend, and taking a variety of classes allows you to get a better feel for what you really like and what you really dislike. During my first and second years of college, I took a variety of classes, which led me to determine what I didn't like. Don't select a major until you are fully certain of what you want to do. Take a variety of classes your first two years, because this is the time to explore what fits best for you. Your assigned academic advisor will help you solidify the process of declaring a major.

PART 3

Avoiding the Sophomore Social Slump

Time Management 201

Time management in college is defined as how you go about regulating and scheduling your time. The key to successful time management is using your time efficiently to balance and complete your academic, personal, and social goals. Additionally, it is finding time to take advantage of all the opportunities that will help you grow and develop. Listed next are time management tips to help you stay organized and focused.

Tip #1: Set Daily and Weekly Goals.

Once you have a sense of direction, you also gain a sense of purpose and tasks seem more meaningful. Setting daily and weekly goals allows you to see the progress you have made over time, so also connect daily and weekly goals with long-term goals. For example, if your goal for the semester is to lose ten pounds, you may wish to go to the gym three times a week. Having structure keeps you focused.

Tip #2: Remember to Take Time for You.

It's okay to say no. If you do not have the energy to help yourself, how can you help others?

Tip #3: Do Not Procrastinate.

Time is your most valuable resource, and procrastinating is something we all are guilty of doing. However, if procrastination is not placed in check, it can come back to hurt you. Choose your time wisely and remember; you must get things done eventually. If you do them sooner, you have more time to correct last-minute mistakes. If you wait until the last minute, that time is no longer available.

Tip #4: Prioritize Your Time.

There are so many new things to do at a new college or university. Give yourself time to become involved with campus life and make friends, but never forget why you are there. Find ways to manage your time and figure out what is most important.

Tip #5: Be Intentional.

Explore new ideas and discover how they relate to you, but don't make decisions too fast. Most decisions are better when they are planned out. Some of the choices you make in college could continue to affect you for the rest of your life. For instance, if you choose to take out a student loan to pay for an expensive car (I have heard stories about this), you eventually have to pay back that loan. Additionally, be strategic in the relationships you form, as they may lead to opportunities you could never imagine. Though sometimes it may be hard to imagine what life will be like years from now, that day does eventually come along.

Things to Consider

- What will I try to avoid this year?
- What can I do differently this year from last year: party less, study more, get out of my room more, see my family more?
- What mistake did I make last year and what did I learn from that mistake?

Finding the Perfect Student Organization

So you didn't get involved your first year. Well, that's okay. It's not too late to get started. Looking for a way to meet people in college? Think about joining a club. There are tons of student organizations on most college campuses, and all of them have something different to offer members. But choosing which group is right can be challenging for a new student on campus. Consider the following tips to find the best fit for you and the variety of campus organizations.

Tip #1: Ask Around.

If you're new on campus, you probably won't know about any student organizations unless you are from the area, so you'll need to do your homework on campus clubs. It's a good idea to learn all you can about a group before you commit to joining. Ask other students which student organizations are the most active and which ones might be best avoided. Your resident advisor or academic advisor is also a good resource for suggestions.

Tip #2: Attend Activities Fairs.

Most colleges hold some sort of activities fair the first week or two of school to introduce new students to the different groups on campus.

If you want to join a club, you'll definitely want to attend the fair. Most organizations provide information about what they do and how to get involved. Club members also attend, so you can see what kind of people are involved in each organization and determine if you're compatible.

Tip #3: Attend Several Meetings.

General meetings of student organizations tend to be open to anyone. If you're thinking about joining a specific group, find out when they hold meetings and drop in. This shouldn't be a problem, especially if it's a larger group.

Tip #4: Look Online.

If you know what type of organization you'd like to join but aren't sure exactly what is out there, check your school's website. Most colleges have an office of student activities dedicated to managing student programs, so check their website for a list of groups on campus. For example, you may want to join an art group but aren't sure what is available. You should be able to find the names and contact information for all art groups online.

Tip #5: Think About Club Sports.

Sports groups are great options for people looking to make friends while also being active. You don't have to be very athletic to join a club sport. Most groups will train new members, and some club sports, like Ultimate Frisbee, are made up of people with varying skill levels. If you want to get involved but are unsure of which group to join, club sports are a good choice.

Tip #6: Extend High School Clubs to College.

Some high school groups and service organizations have college counterparts. If you enjoyed being in a certain organization in high school, do some research to see if there's a similar college group out there for you. For example, student government is an organization always found in both high school and college. If you don't like a club you join, you can always leave it, so you really have nothing to lose. Get out there and get involved on campus!

Make a list of 3-4 organizations you are interested in joining:

1.
2.
3.
4.

Things to Consider

- What do I like to do for fun?
- What organizations did I join last year? Did they meet my expectations? Why or why not?
- What organizations will I join this year?
- What am I looking for in an organization?
- What gifts and talents do I have to offer?

PART 4

Avoiding the Sophomore Debt Slump

Staying Out of Debt

It's now one year down and three to four years to go before you complete your first bachelor's degree. Congratulations on getting through your first year, but have you stopped to think how you will get through the next three to four years?

This chapter is filled with tips to help make your second year more affordable. Let's begin with 16 highly effective tips.

Tip #1: Re-apply for Federal Financial Aid.

Even if you don't think you qualify, re-apply for federal financial aid. Filing a FAFSA doesn't cost a thing. Also, consider that your parent or guardian status could have changed and, therefore, you may qualify for more money or better loans.

Tip #2: Look Everywhere.

Grants and scholarships can be found anywhere: in your community, your parents' employers, religious centers, local organizations such as service clubs, businesses and local government agencies. Explore all opportunities.

Tip #3: Live Off Campus.

Perhaps you've had enough of the on-campus experience and want to live off campus. This may save you a lot of money, particularly if you are close enough to live at home. Also consider a co-op situation. Co-op housing is where students exchange low rent in exchange for a few hours of work a week. Not all colleges offer co-ops, but it's definitely worth exploring.

Tip #4: Touch Base with Various Campus Offices.

Colleges have a way of helping the hardworking and deserving find money for college. The Honors Department, Financial Aid, Alumni Association, Student Support offices, and even professors can suggest money-saving opportunities. Some scholarship recipients don't return after their first year, and the organization still needs to give the money to someone. So, why not to you? Federally funded scholarships, especially, must be awarded, so even if you don't fit all of the criteria, it's still a good idea to pursue these opportunities.

Tip #5: Sign Up for Scholarship Websites.

Be sure to sign up for free services like www.fastweb.com, and continue to stay active.

One of the biggest mistakes most college students make is not continuing to apply for scholarships long after they have received them and been admitted to the institution. Remember, the pursuit of your college degree is an ongoing process, and you should continue to apply for funds to pay for school.

Tip #6: Attend Classes at a Community College or Take the CLEP.

Taking classes at a community college may save you money, rather than taking more expensive classes elsewhere. As a sophomore, you will continue to take general education courses and electives that can be taken at the community college level. The only drawback in taking classes at a community college is that you may need to pay for them out of your pocket.

Tip #7: Petition Your Financial Aid Office.

Write a letter to your financial aid director asking for more money. This may not work in all instances, but if you are a good student, you will have a better chance of them increasing your award amount. However, if you have not lived up to your promise, it will hurt your case considerably. Either way, it's a good idea to ask for more money, because you never know. Tell the director of any circumstances that affect your need for more money, such as big medical bills, parents becoming unemployed, or other unusual circumstances.

Tip #8: Get a Part-time Job.

Obviously this is not the sexiest choice, but your aim is to get your debt down. Also, if you've never worked a day in your life, it will be a great way to get work experience.

Tip #9: Monthly Payment Plan.

If you are not already doing this, this option is the way to go. It allows you to break down the debt payment month-to-month instead of trying to pay it all at once. Check with your school for more information.

Tip #10: Hold a Fundraiser.

Having a fundraiser is by far the least conventional idea of all. However, considering this tough economic climate, all options are on the table. Besides, what cause could be better than you receiving an education?

Tip #11: Change Your Meal Plan.

Most college students spend a lot of money ordering food or eating at local restaurants. Sure, eating on campus and in the dining hall is convenient, but it can be costly. If you don't plan to eat 3-4 times a day, you may want to change your meal plan. It can very well save you thousands of dollars.

Tip #12: Become a Resident Assistant.

A Resident Assistant is a non-first-year

student who helps to build community in residential housing. Typically, resident assistants (or resident advisors, each school has different titles) are compensated with room and/or board in exchange for services. Being an RA can shave off room and board expenses so you can focus on tuition and other costs.

Tip #13: If it's Too Hot in the Kitchen, Transfer.

I don't advocate transferring institutions, but I also don't believe in debt. If you risk going into debt, you may want to consider transferring to a cheaper institution to get a bit of relief. Unless you've already selected a major that only your present school offers, transferring may not be such a bad idea, especially if it means you will not be in a ton of debt after school.

Tip #14: Shop for Cheaper Loans.

Just because you are given a student loan by a school does not mean that you must take it.

Let's say your institution offers you a loan at 8% interest, but you decide to shop around and find another loan at 5%. Well, the math is clear; you'll save quite a bit over the life of the loan. It's always wise to shop around, especially with loans, because it's not so much the principal amount borrowed that causes people to go into major debt; it's the interest.

Tip #15: Rent Your Textbooks.

If you don't know by now, renting your textbooks is the best way to go. It can save you an average of $400-$600 dollars a year on the cost of brand new textbooks. You be the judge. Besides, are you really going to read that history book again after you've taken the class?

Tip #16: Change Insurance Policies.

Do your parents have an insurance plan that will cover you? While campus insurance plans are certainly convenient, unless you have an ongoing illness or are subject to reoccurring accidents, you may want to consider getting on your parents' or guardian's plan.

Money Management 101

Sophomores need to educate themselves about money management, especially careful and disciplined use of credit cards. Financial worries are taken care of by credit cards, and in a way, credit lends a financial hand to students, standing by them in their most critical money needs. But this doesn't mean that credit cards can be used in a haphazard manner. As you grow, your needs rise, but be mindful to use these handy financial aids wisely to avert more unwanted debt.

Tip #1: Prioritize Needs Over Wants.

College students must learn to tend to their primary needs first before fulfilling their wants. For example, an effective academic curriculum is obviously a primary need. On the other hand, eating at a restaurant is a want, which can be avoided to better manage your money. Placing a priority on your needs can save money that otherwise might be wasted on unnecessary wants, like partying with friends or watching movies.

Tip #2: Stay Away from Things Beyond Your Reach.

Most college students crave owning things that are too costly, just to fulfill their desires. Understand your needs first. As you proceed with your academics, learn to respect money and know where best to spend it. Learning how to manage money helps you to know your financial limits so you can start saving for your future.

Tip #3: Set Up a Budget.

First, identify your sources of income. Students primarily receive financial help from parents; they generate secondary income by working part-time. Then calculate your monthly expenses. Next, set aside part of your income (maybe 5%) for savings. Then deduct the expenses from savings and income to find out how much money you have to spend for other needs or wants. Be realistic and truthful!

Tip #4: Encourage Financial Discipline.

After you have planned a budget, **stick to it at any cost**. This is vital for effective money management. Avoid eating at restaurants and develop the habit of preparing meals on your own. You may not be allowed to use the college cafeteria for cooking, but you can probably cook in your apartment, which will be less expensive than eating out. Purchase used textbooks, usually available at discounted rates. Utilize your dorm room for watching movies every weekend, rather than spend money at movie theaters with friends.

Tip #5: Understand Your Responsibilities.

Maturing college students should learn to differentiate between gross and net income. Estimate expenses you are likely to incur related to rent, groceries, car, insurance and utilities. You may even obtain health insurance. Use your credit card wisely, and try not to invite bad credit to your name, which will make getting large future purchases quite difficult.

Tip #6: Supervise Your Checking Account.

College students should know how much money they need each week, on average. They need to restrict frequent trips to the ATM. Visit the ATM to draw money only once a week, and if you have one, use a debit card to escape ATM charges. Wherever possible, use an online option for money transfers and bill paying. Protect your account by using a bank overdraft facility.

Tip #7: Consider a Job, Tuition Assistance, and Internship.

To help manage money, some students may take on a job. Try to acquire a job related to your field. Providing tuition assistance will help you to earn money; you may save the money you get from parents. Students may even take up internship, either part-time or full-time, which helps to avoid debt and provides better financial controls. These are the most beneficial ways students can manage money while in college.

Tip #8: Invest in the Future.

It's advisable for college students to:

- Have money deducted either from their checking account or their paycheck.
- Build a fund for meeting unforeseen expenses and auto repairs.
- Know the importance of mutual funds, which compound earnings over a lifetime.
- Follow an investment plan and invest money into it every month.

Accumulated money helps students to achieve bigger academic goals and to never feel financially crippled in life.

PART 5

What Else Should I Consider This Year?

Unlike your first year, you have already begun to establish yourself. You are already invested in the institution, and as a result, you have more freedom, in terms of privileges.

You can live off campus and have a car on campus. You are no longer just taking general education courses; you can begin taking more electives related to your proposed major.

You may have other concerns that are not only academic. Financial assistance from your first year may not be renewable. You may not have the same roommate from last year. You may need to bring up your GPA, decide on a major, or get a better idea of what you want to declare. Though you are still learning how to balance your schedule and all that comes with it, professors, family and peers expect more of you.

How do you begin to address the concerns and challenges you face this year? This section offers advice to make your sophomore year even more successful and enriching by interning, studying aboard, service learning, or living off campus. This advice can render major benefits.

Interning, Studying Abroad, or Service Learning Opportunities?

Interning

Internships are opportunities for students to combine a career related work experience with academic coursework. Most internships occur during the summer, but depending on their guidelines, you can work some during the school year. Establish a good relationship with various offices, professors, and other professionals. It can pay off for you when internships are awarded.

Bulletin boards that you see all over campus are good places to find internship opportunities. You also may want to utilize social media like Referral Key, LinkedIn, Facebook, and Twitter.

If you go to the career services office in a timely manner, you may be able to find other opportunities. While there, staff members will help you create or polish your resume, as well as give you interviewing and job hunting tips.

Begin looking for an internship around October or November. Many students make the mistake of looking for an internship at the beginning of the summer or late April. By this time, internship opportunities are usually no longer available. As the saying goes, "the early bird gets the worm."

Finding internships are all about preparation, patience and persistence. As some require recommendations, enlist people who can give you a *favorable* recommendation early.

<u>Steps for Securing an Internship</u>

1. **Start early.** Students should start their search for an internship at least two to three months before they would like to begin.
2. **Make a list of companies you'll like to work with.** Identify target internships. Before you approach these companies, be sure that your resume and cover letter are up to par. You can go to the Career Service office to get help with your resume and interview.
3. **Make sure your internship is valid.** Websites like <u>InternshipRatings.com</u> and <u>InternshipKing.com</u> both offer ratings of internships.
4. **Apply for your internship.** Make sure you stand out. Remember, employers hire people that stand out (in a good way).

5. Network, network, network! Even after you get an internship, you should always continue to network. You never know the type of opportunities that will come your way as a result.

Studying Abroad

Perhaps one of the biggest regrets of my undergraduate experience was not participating in a **study abroad** program. If your institution has a program or an international programs office, I highly recommend taking advantage of this opportunity. Besides gaining a greater appreciation of other cultures and a greater global perspective, studying abroad looks very good on your **résumé**. Also, you may not have this opportunity for such an adventure later in life.

If you are unsure if you can afford it, the amount you normally pay each semester comes close to covering the amount required for the experience. If you receive financial aid and are eligible to receive a **pell grant**, programs like the

Benjamin Gillman Scholarship program award money to students demonstrating financial need.

Pros and cons of studying aboard include:

Pros:

- It gives you a boarder world prospective.
- It looks good on your résumé.
- You will be connected globally.
- It strengthens your foreign language skills.
- It could lead to other international opportunities.
- You can immerse yourself in another culture with support from the institution.
- It's a once-in-a-lifetime experience.
- Assistance is available.

Cons:

- Associated costs with the trip can add up.
- Homesickness.

- You're disconnected from family and friends.
- The trip may set you back from your graduation time frame.

You may also want to consider the following questions:

1. Where would I like to study aboard?
2. What other costs are associated with this experience, like immunization shots, a passport, travel insurance?
3. Will this study aboard experience benefit my career?
4. Do I plan to do this with friends? What if we're not placed in the same country?
5. What kinds of opportunities can potentially come from this experience?
6. Do I speak and understand the language of this country?
7. What do I expect to gain from this experience?
8. Is this country facing any current social or economic crisis?

9. Is this country foreign-friendly?
10. Can I afford this experience? (Write down your potential expenses.)
11. What supporting documents will I need?
12. When I'm not in class, how do I plan to spend my time?
13. Where will I stay and will I be comfortable with the accommodations?
14. Will this experience mean more time at this school?
15. What are my top five choices, and why?
16. How did other students feel about their study aboard experience?

Overall, studying aboard is a great opportunity for you to see the world. While it may not be for every student, it's still a good idea to check out your options. You must decide what this experience means to you and if the advantages outweigh the benefits, or vice versa. As with all things, take time to carefully think through this decision.

Service Learning Opportunities

Service learning is a wonderful option. It combines your interest in your field with providing community service for the betterment of the community. Below are some tips on how to find available service learning opportunities.

☑ Ask Your Instructor: Keep in mind that service learning is valuable even if it doesn't relate to your choice of study. Your instructor may have some ideas or know places where your services could be used. The main concept is twofold; you want to be able to service your community, and at the same time learn something.

☑ Ask Fellow Students: Ask around, as many of your fellow students will be looking for the same service learning opportunity as you. They may have information they can share with you.

☑ Student Volunteer Services: You will find that most colleges have something like this in place. A great idea is to check out the opportunities they have, as businesses and individuals may contact the college asking for interested volunteers. There is usually an assortment of opportunities both on and off campus.

☑ Career Services Department: You may find some interesting opportunities here. When you complete your schooling and go into the workforce, you'll find that it's very competitive. It's sad, but in most cases having just an education is generally not enough. Most employers are looking for individuals who have gone above and beyond, and this includes taking advantage of service learning opportunities. Usually, it's helpful if they are career related, but they don't have to be. There are always businesses and individuals that love to have young college students in their midst sharing their knowledge.

☑ Part of Your Curriculum: All too often you will have a class that has a service learning component built into it. This is also a great opportunity and will more than likely be course related, so you know it's something you will like.

☑ Make Your Own: Nothing is stopping you from making your own service learning opportunity. For example, you can initiate this with a place in your community that is also related to your studies. Most places will welcome the chance to have you there, and it is a win-win situation for everyone. Also, you may want to check out servicelearning.org.

There are many tips on how to make the most of your schooling, and it's in your best interest to look into a service learning experience. Aside from giving you a different outlook on life and a fresh perspective, it can enhance your chances when looking for employment.

Living Off Campus as a Sophomore

Depending on your institution's existing policies, you will not necessarily be bound to live on campus in campus housing. Therefore, before securing housing for the upcoming school year, you should definitely think about whether or not you want to live on-campus or off-campus.

If you plan to live <u>on campus</u>, you can expect the following pros and cons:

- A more structured environment (rules, more accountability)
- Easier access to campus resources (Internet, library, laundry facilities)
- Greater opportunities to get involved in campus organizations
- Instant community (social and extracurricular)
- Easier access to classes
- A greater opportunity to meet more people
- Limited privacy

- Limited Internet downloading and file sharing
- Adherence to guest, visitation, or curfew policies
- Sharing common places (study area, bathroom)
- Possible relocation when school is out

If you plan to live <u>off campus</u>, you can expect the following pros and cons:

- More privacy
- Less structured environment
- Campus commute
- No guest, visitation, or curfew policies
- Limited opportunities to get involved
- Less access to classes
- Limited access to campus resources
- Private common places (bathroom, kitchen)
- No relocation in summer months (you may be able to sign a lease for the entire year)

I Can't Decide…Are There Other Options?

If you like the conveniences of living on campus but the benefits of living off campus, you should consider an on-campus apartment (if this option exists). On campus apartments or houses are usually not available to first-year students. Contact the institution's Housing or Residence Life department for more information about alternate housing options.

<u>Things to Consider</u>

1. What are you looking for in a new apartment?
2. What are looking for in your new community?
3. Does your current community have any of these qualities?

List five reasons to move off campus:

1.
2.

3.

4.

5.

List five reasons to stay on campus:

1.

2.

3.

4.

5.

List the names of 2-5 friends you think would make good potential roommates. Why?

1.

2.

3.

4.

5.

A Quick Reminder When Securing Housing

If you plan to live on campus again, you should contact the institution's housing department as soon as possible to begin the process of securing a room for the upcoming school year, quarter, or semester. Because you are already in the system, it will be a matter of formality at this point.

Every school has a different process that usually involves some kind of lottery. The goal is to give priority to upper class students and generally make it as easy as possible for everyone else. As long as you are in good financial standing with the institution, you should be able to maintain your spot. Since every institution functions differently, find out each institution's procedures regarding reservations and securing housing.

GLOSSARY

Academic Advising: Assistance to students in choosing courses by providing information about majors, various academic programs, and academic policies and procedures.

Academic Advisor: A faculty or professional staff member trained to help students with selecting classes, scheduling, and choosing a major and/or minor. Advisors may also assist students in establishing their educational and career goals.

Academic Dismissal: Dismissal from a college or program for not maintaining the required grade point average (GPA). Dismissal indicates that a student is no longer a member of the institution's community.

Academic Standing: A student's academic standing is determined by the number of credit hours attempted and the number of quality points earned. There are typically five categories of academic standing: good standing, academic warning, academic probation, academic suspension, and academic dismissal. If you are on some form of financial aid, it is affected by your academic standing.

Sophomore Success

Academic Warning: The status assigned to a student with a cumulative GPA of less than 2.0.

Accelerated study: A college program of study completed in less time than is usually required, most often by attending classes in summer or by taking extra courses during the regular academic terms.

ACT: A standardized achievement examination for college admissions in the United States. The ACT measures high school students' general educational development and their ability to complete college-level work with the multiple-choice tests covering four skill areas: English, mathematics, reading, and science.

Adjunct Faculty: Part-time certified instructors.

Admission: Acceptance of an applicant for enrollment.

Advanced Placement (AP): Exams offered at the high school level only. University credits may be acquired through the AP examinations. These credits may be used to fill General Education requirements and may also be accepted as equivalent to specific courses.

Affidavit of Educational Purpose: A document signed by a student who is awarded one or more forms of federal financial aid.

Alumni: Graduates or former students of the institution.

Articulation: A term that is used to indicate that a course taken at another institution is equivalent to a course at the institution in which a student is planning to transfer.

Articulation Agreements: Documents that formally acknowledge how credits or degrees from other institutions equate to courses and requirements.

Assistant Resident Director: A live-in paraprofessional who assists in managing a residence hall. Assistant Resident Directors are usually full-time graduate students.

Associate Degree: A degree granted by a college or university after the satisfactory completion of the equivalent of a two-year, full-time program of study.

Audit: Registration in a course without credit or grade. Class attendance is required.

Award Letter: A letter from a college's financial aid office explaining the financial aid package that the school is offering a student. It outlines the amount and types of aid that will be awarded. The student must either accept or reject all or part of the award.

Bachelor's Degree: A degree in an academic discipline which typically requires completion of a minimum of 120 semester credit hours.

Board: A term used for the meal plan (as in, room and board) at the university.

Bulletin: A publication that lists the schedule of courses for an upcoming academic term. At some institutions, bulletins are considered the school's catalogue.

Bursar: An official in charge of funds, as at a college or university. Normally, this is the office you go to in order to pay your bills.

Call Number: A code that identifies a specific course.

Career Services: An office that is dedicated to assisting students with résumé writing, interviewing skills, and job placement. Typically, career service offices offer assessment to help students discover their strengths and weaknesses with regard to choosing a major or finding a career.

Cashier: The financial officer of the university who receives payment of tuition and miscellaneous fees.

Certificate: A document certifying that one has fulfilled the requirements of and may practice in a certain vocation.

Class Rank: Student's ranking of being a freshman (less than 30 credits), sophomore (30-59 credits), junior (60-89 credits), or senior (90 or more credits), based on the number of college-level credit hours earned.

Closed Class: A class that has been filled by the maximum number of students allowed for that class.

Cognate: A course, or courses, related in some way to courses in a major. Cognates may be, and often are, courses outside the department of the degree program.

College: An academic division in a university. A college is composed of academic departments and is headed by a dean; for example, the College of Arts and Sciences or the College of Natural Sciences.

College Catalogue: Lists every department and course available at the institution.

College Level Examination Program (CLEP): A standardized examination in college-level subject matter. Subject examinations cover material offered in specific advanced-level courses. Credits may be acquired through the CLEP examinations. If a student passes the CLEP examination for a specific subject, they will receive college credit.

College Work Study: A form of financial aid based on need that provides students with paid employment while in school.

Cooperative Education: A program that provides for alternative class attendance and employment in business, industry, or government. Students typically are paid for their work.

Cooperative Housing: College-owned, operated, or affiliated housing in which students share room and board expenses and participate in household chores to reduce living expenses.

Commencement: A term used to refer to the graduation ceremony held in the last month of the school's spring, winter or summer semester.

Commercial Loan: A loan made through a bank or other lending institution for educational purposes as well as for a house, a car, or other consumer purchases.

Common Application: A college admission application that students may use to apply to any of 321 member colleges and universities in the United States. A Common Application reduces the workload of students who would otherwise have to complete separate applications to several colleges.

Commuter Student: One who lives at home and travels to the college.

Competency Test: A test that is used to determine if a student has the acquired knowledge of a college-level course. These tests are also referred to as placement test.

Complete Withdrawal: The process of withdrawing from all courses before a semester has ended. Students usually explore this option when they have a circumstance that does not allow them to continue.

Composite Major: When elements of two major programs are combined into one major program. For example, the Elementary Education/Special Education major is an approved composite of two different majors.

Concentration: A concentration (or option or emphasis) is a group of courses that are more similar to one another than to others in the degree program. For example, a student can major in History but their concentration is Early World History.

Concurrent Enrollment: When a high school student is enrolled in a university course for which the student simultaneously receives high school and university credit.

Continuing Education: Courses that students can take without pursuing a degree.

Continuing Education Unit (CEU): Recognition for participation in a non-credit program or workshop at a college or university.

Sophomore Success

Convocation: An opening ceremony to welcome new students. At some institutions, it is a lecture series that happens either at the beginning and/or during the academic year. At some institutions, convocations are mandatory.

Co-op: Two or more related internship work experiences.

Course Fee: A fee that is attached to a specific course, in addition to tuition.

Course Load: The number of credit hours carried by a student during a given semester. Generally, students need to average a minimum of 12 credit hours per semester in order to be considered full time.

Course Reference Number (CRN): A five-digit number used to select a specific course, lab, and/or recitation.

Corequisite: A course that must be taken at the same time as another course.

Credit Hour: A unit of academic credit measured in semester hours or quarter hours. One credit hour usually represents one hour of class time per week.

Credit Load: The total number of credits for which a student registers during a semester or session.

Cross-listed Course: A cross-listed course is interdisciplinary in nature and, therefore, is listed as a course offered under two or more departments.

Cumulative Index: A number that represents the average of all earned grades.

Curriculum: A series of courses that meet a particular academic or vocational goal.

Deadline: The date by which certain information must be received by any given office or unit.

Dean: A college or university administrative official. An academic dean usually heads a college within the university. However, some deans meet with students regarding disciplinary issues.

Declaration of Major: At some institutions, a process whereby students formally notify the Registrar's Office of the major that they choose to include in their degree program.

Deferred Admission: When a student is accepted for a specific term but chooses to defer his or her admission until a future term.

Degree: A title bestowed as official recognition for the completion of a curriculum. The bachelor's degree is the first-level degree granted normally upon completion of a four-year course of study in a given field. The master's degree is an advanced degree that requires at least one additional year beyond the bachelor's degree. The doctor's degree, or doctorate, is an advanced degree requiring at least three years beyond the bachelor's degree. The professional degrees of Juris Doctor (a law degree) and Doctor of Medicine require three and four years, respectively, beyond the pre-professional curricula. The honorary degree is bestowed in recognition of outstanding merit or achievement without reference to the fulfillment of academic course requirements.

Degree Audit: A summary of academic progress showing courses completed and courses needed. An official degree audit is normally done for graduating students once they have completed their application for graduation.

Degree Student: A student who has been admitted to a degree category and is seeking a bachelor's, master's, or doctoral degree in a planned course of study.

Department: A division of a college that offers instruction in a particular branch of knowledge, for example the Department of English.

Department Head: The administrative head of an academic department, sometimes referred to as department chair.

Dependent Student: A student who lives with and is at least partially supported by parents or a guardian and who is claimed by them as a dependent for income tax purposes or one to whom these conditions applied in the academic year prior to applying for financial aid.

Diploma Mill: A term used to describe an organization that awards academic degrees and diplomas usually without recognition by legitimate and official accrediting bodies.

Discipline: A subject area; for example, English, Spanish, religious studies, and elementary education.

Disenrollment: The process by which a student is dropped from all their courses due to non-payment of tuition or other university related action (e.g. suspension).

Dissertation: A written thesis by a candidate for a doctoral degree.

Doctorate: An academic degree of the highest level. It is usually earned after you have completed a master's degree, although you can begin working on it after having a bachelor's degree. The time to complete this degree depends upon if you are full-time or part-time. If you are full-time, it normally takes 7-8 years to complete. Although the Ph.D. (**Doctor of Philosophy**) is the most commonly known doctorate degree, there are well over twenty types. When a person earns a doctorate degree, he/she then are referred to with their title (e.g., Dr. James Taylor or James Taylor, Ph.D.) Professionals who hold a Ph.D. are not the same as M.Ds (medical doctors).

Drop/Add: The process used if students need to change a schedule for which they have already registered. This process usually can only occur during the first or second week of the semester.

Dual Major: Any two majors that are completed at the same time; also referred to as double major.

Elective: A course that the student may study by choice but which may or may not be required for the student's particular degree.

Expected Family Contribution (EFC): An amount, determined by a formula that is specified by law, that indicates how much of a family's financial resources should be available to help pay for school. Factors such as taxable and non-taxable income, assets (such as savings and checking accounts), and benefits (for example, unemployment or Social Security) are all considered in this calculation. The EFC is used in determining eligibility for federal needs-based aid.

Faculty: Academic staff of a university: professors, lectures, and/or researchers.

Family Educational Rights and Privacy Act (FERPA): A law that (1) provides that students will have access to inspect or review their educational records and (2) protects the rights of a student to privacy by limiting access to the educational record without express written consent. These rights transfer to the student when he or she reaches the age of 18 or attends a school beyond the high school level.

Federal Family Education Loan Program (FFELP): Education loans provided by private lenders and guaranteed by the federal government. Subsidized and unsubsidized Federal Stafford Loans and parent PLUS loans are included in this program.

Fees: Charges that cover costs not associated with tuition. In many cases, fees cover costs associated with student activities (clubs, student organizations, athletics, and special events).

Financial Aid Money: Scholarships, grants, loans, and work study that is awarded to students to help reduce the cost of college.

Financial Aid Package: The total amount of financial aid a student receives. For example, grants, loans, or work-study are combined in a "package" to help meet the student's needs.

Financial Assistance Award: The total package consisting of a combination of scholarships, loans, and part-time employment.

Financial Assistance Counselor: A staff person who works in the financial aid office who reviews a student's application, awards financial assistance, and helps the student and parents in all aspects of financing their education.

Financial Aid Transcript (FAT): Designed for use by upper class students transferring to a new institution, a document required from each school previously attended whether financial assistance was received or not. This document is required by the school at which a student is applying for financial assistance.

Financial Need: The difference between the cost of attendance and the estimated family contribution. This amount is the total eligibility for financial assistance from all sources, and it is used in determining the total amount of a financial assistance award.

First Generation College Student (FGCS): College students whose parents have had no previous postsecondary experience.

First Time in College (FTIC): A first-year student entering with less than 12 hours of college credit.

Forbearance: A postponement of loan payments, granted by a lender or creditor, for a temporary period. This is granted to give the borrower time to make up for overdue payments.

Fraternity: A male student society formed for either academic and/or social purposes, into which members are initiated by invitation and/or by voluntarily, sign up themselves. The goal of most fraternities is to promote goodwill among its members and a social network among its members. Fraternities are usually named by two or three Greek letters. Fraternities are also known as Greek-letter societies.

Free Application for Federal Student Aid (FAFSA): The federal financial assistance application. This must be completed by all students who wish to be considered for financial assistance.

Full-Time Student: Normally a student registered for 12 or more credit hours during a semester.

General Education Requirements: A set of requirements that all candidates for a college degree, regardless of major, must satisfy.

Grace Period: The six-month period between the time you leave school and the time you must start paying back your loan.

Grade Point Average (GPA): Total number of grade points received for each grade divided by total number of credits attempted.

Graduate Student: A student who has earned a bachelor's degree and is enrolled for advanced work in a graduate school.

Graduation Audit: A formal, required evaluation of the student's academic record and program of study to determine the student's eligibility for graduation. The audit, initiated by a student's application for graduation, determines whether all university, degree, and program requirements have been met satisfactorily.

Grant: A type of financial assistance award that does not need to be repaid by the student.

Greek Letter Societies: Organizations that include academic honor societies, and fraternities or sororities.

Gross Income: The total income of a family, including salaries, wages, interest, social security benefits, and any other taxable and nontaxable income.

Helicopter Parent (slang): A parent who is very attentive to his or her child or children, when they start in college or university. Helicopter parents have the tendency to hover and not allow their child to make independent decisions. This term has been popularized by university officials in the last couple of years, due to the rise of more millennial age students starting postsecondary institutions.

Hold: An official action taken by the institution possibly to prevent student registration or receipt of grades and transcripts until a student satisfies a requirement. For example, a registration hold is placed on a student until he or she has met his or her financial obligations.

Honors Program: A program for high-achieving students within an institution.

Incomplete Grade (*I*): A temporary grade that may be assigned when a student is unable to complete all of the work in a course due to extenuating circumstances but not due to poor performance.

Independent Student: A student who is not financially dependent on any other person, expect a spouse, for support.

Independent Study: Credits earned by working on an independent research or reading project supervised by a faculty member.

In-State Student: A student who is a legal resident of the state in which he/she attends school.

Institutional Student Information Report (ISIR): The Institutional Student Information Report (ISIR) is the name for the electronic version of Student Aid Reports (SARs) delivered to schools by the FAFSA processors.

Interdisciplinary: Designating a combination of subject matter from two or more disciplines within a course or program.

Internship: An opportunity for students to combine a career related work experience with academic coursework. In an internship, a student can gain supervised practical experience in a professional field. Internships may or may not count for academic credit, it is based on previous arrangements.

Lab: A class whereby students perform experiments in a laboratory. Labs are usually required for natural science courses such as Biology, Chemistry, Physics, etc. They are frequently offered concurrently with lecture courses in the same subject.

Lecture: When an instructor speaks to the class for the entire class period with little or no class interaction.

Living Learning Communities (LLC): Communities that are established to provide special settings where academic successes are combined with residential experiences. Living-Learning Communities are normally housed on a floor in a residence hall and focus on a theme, major, or other special interest. They usually support the interest of community members in conjunction with special academic or social programming.

Loan: Loaned money that must be repaid over a period. Typically, a student must repay the loan amount plus interest.

Major: An academic subject chosen as a field of specialization, requiring a specific course of study.

Matriculation: The process of applying and gaining acceptance into a degree program at a college or university.

Mentor: An individual that is more experienced who guides and helps another individual.

Merit-Based Financial Aid: This kind of financial aid is given to students who meet requirements not related to financial needs. Most merit-based aid is awarded based on academic performance or potential and is given in the form of scholarships or grants.

Minor: The field of second emphasis. Fewer semester hours' credit is required for a minor than for a major.

Need-based Financial Aid: Financial aid given to students who are determined to be in financial need of assistance based on their income and assets and their families' income and assets.

Needs Analysis: A process of reviewing a student's financial assistance application to determine the amount of financial assistance for which a student is eligible. Completing a needs analysis form is the required first step in applying for most types of financial assistance.

Noncustodial Parent's Statement: When parents of an applicant are separated or divorced, financial information from both parents is requested. The Noncustodial Parent's Statement is a form for the noncustodial parent to use to report this information.

Non-Degree Seeking: A student enrolled in courses for credit that is not recognized by the institution as seeking a degree or formal award.

Non-Resident Alien: A person who is not a citizen or national of the United States and who is in this country on a visa or temporary basis and does not have the right to remain indefinitely.

Nontraditional Student: A college student who is older than the typical undergraduate college student (usually aged 17-23). Normally, nontraditional college students are students who return to school after years of being away or older adults who attend college in the evening or on a part-time basis.

Orientation: A program that is designed to enable new students to have a smooth transition into the institution. Although not all orientations are the same, at most orientations, students have the opportunity to learn about academic and social expectations, meet other students, learn about the institution's services and resources, get acquainted with the campus, and meet with campus administrators.

Outside Scholarships: Scholarships from organizations outside the university such as corporations, foundations, service clubs, and local organizations. Often these scholarships are awarded directly to the student.

Overload: A process in which a student may obtain permission from their advisor to register for an increased credit load (typically 18 or more credits).

Part-time: The status of a student registered for fewer than usually twelve credits during a regular semester or quarter.

Pass/Fail: An option given in some classes whereby students may choose to take a course on a pass/fail basis.

A letter grade is not given; the student either passes or fails.

Pell Grant: A federal student aid program for undergraduates, for undergraduate students, first baccalaureate degree only. The amount of the award ranges from $400 to $4,050, subject to Congressional appropriations, and is reduced for students who enroll part-time. It is only given to students who demonstrate financial need.

Perkins Loan: A low fixed interest federal loan for both undergraduate and graduate students with exceptional financial need.

Personal Statement: Essays used by admissions committees to learn more about their applicants. Personal statements are also known as the application essay. Personal statements are usually required by schools that are competitive. They are very common for graduate and professional school admission.

PIN Number: A personal identification number that is used as a password. The pin number is usually required in order to register online.

Placement Test: A test given to determine the appropriate level at which to place a student in certain courses. Placement tests are usually required before you can enroll in a class.

PLUS Loan: Loans that enable parents with good credit histories to borrow the education expenses of each child who is a dependent undergraduate student enrolled at least part-time.

Portfolio: An arrangement of projects, documents and/or artwork that is used in some majors and degree programs for admission decisions, assessment, career placement, or graduation requirements.

Postsecondary Institution: Any proprietary or vocational school, college, or university that offers education and training to students beyond the high school level. It is also referred to as higher education.

Practicum: A course of study designed especially for the preparation of teachers and clinicians. A practicum involves the supervised practical application of previously studied classes and theory.

Prerequisite: A course that must be completed prior to taking another course.

Priority Registration: The order in which students may register for classes. A priority registration schedule indicates the earliest possible day a student may register for classes.

Sophomore Success

Professor: A college teacher of the highest rank. At a college or university, there are assistant, associate, visiting, and full professors.

Probation (Academic): An academic status indicating that a student's cumulative index is below 2.0 GPA.

Promissory Note: A contract stating the terms of agreement of a promise by one party to pay a sum of money to the other. The promissory note usually has to be signed before you can take out a student loan.

Quarter System: The division of the academic year into four equal parts.

Reading Day: Usually the day before and/or the week of final exams, when no exams or classes are scheduled.

Recitation: A class period especially in association with and for review of a lecture.

Registrar: The administrative officer who maintains enrollment records and certifies the academic standing, as well as the fulfillment of graduation requirements, for all enrolled students.

Registration: The act of enrolling in classes.

Remedial Course: A course that will not satisfy degree requirements, are not transferable, and are not calculated in a student's grade point average. They usually serve as a prerequisite class for credited classes.

Residence Hall: A building that houses a formal and/or informal living and learning community that is part of the larger academic institution. Although many people refer to residence halls as dorms, the environment of the building is not just were students sleep. It is the place where the majority of learning outside of the classroom takes place.

Residency: A classification for tuition purposes. In-state residents pay lower tuition than nonresidents.

Resident Assistant: The Resident Assistant (RA) is a full-time student who is employed by the university or college to live on campus and assigned to a particular floor or area in the Residence Halls. The RA assists residents in meeting their educational, interpersonal, and social needs relative to their living environment. They also assist with crisis intervention and provide educational and social activities for residents; also referred to as resident advisor, community assistant, fellow, etc.

Resident Director: A live-in educator who manages a residence hall. Resident Directors are full-time professionals who usually supervise Resident Assistants. They are also involved in advising students, crisis intervention, completing administrative tasks (room transfers, maintenance issues, keys), setting limits on the floor and throughout the building, and implementing floor and building events (programs). Additionally, at most institutions, Resident Directors meet with students who violate hall and/or university policies (noise, alcohol, drug, etc.). Some schools also refer to Resident Directors as Hall Directors, Area Coordinators, etc.

Résumé: A document containing a summary or listing of previous or relevant job experience and education, usually for the purpose of obtaining an interview when seeking employment. Students should try to have a résumé done no later than the end of their freshman year.

Reserve Officers Training Corps (ROTC): A scholarship program offered by many colleges and universities wherein the military covers the cost of tuition, fees, and textbooks and also provides a monthly allowance. In exchange, scholarship recipients participate in summer training while in college and fulfill a service commitment after college.

Rolling Admissions: A policy where admissions offices review and decide on applications as they are received, until there are no openings left in the entering class. When a school has a rolling admissions policy, they usually do not have a deadline for applications; however, it is on a first come, first serve basis.

Sophomore Success

Rush: A drive by a Greek letter society on a college campus to recruit new members. Depending upon the college or university, rushes usually take place during the beginning of the school year.

SAT: A standardized test used for college admission in the United States. The SAT consists of three major sections: <u>Mathematics</u>, Critical <u>Reading</u>, and <u>Writing</u>. Each section receives a score on the scale of 200–800.

Security Deposit: Money paid upfront in order to protect the provider of a product or service against damage or nonpayment by the buyer. For example, landlords usually require a security deposit of one month's rent when a tenant signs a lease to cover the possibility that the tenant will move out without paying the last month's rent or that the tenant will inflict substantial damage on the property while living there. Before you can move into campus housing you must submit a security deposit with your application.

Service Learning: A fairly new experiential learning experience that balances the needs of student and community members. Additionally, service learning connects service and learning through a reflective process. Students tend to gain a sense of social responsibility, increased intellectual development, and career development.

Scholarship: Student financial aid based on academic achievement, need, or a combination of factors. Scholarships do not have to be repaid.

Semester: A 14 or 15 week period of study. There are two semesters in an academic year.

Sorority: A female student society formed for either academic and/or social purposes, into which members are initiated by invitation, or they voluntarily sign up themselves. The goal of most sororities is to promote sisterhood and a social network among its members. Sororities are usually named by two or three Greek letters. Sororities are also considered Greek-letter societies.

Specialization: An approved area of study, having a specific curriculum within a particular graduate degree.

Stafford Loans: Stafford loans are student loans. They are provided by banks and are federally regulated.

Student Activities: An office or department at a college or university that provides opportunities for students to be involved in the life of the school. The office usually oversees all organizations to which students are members.

Student Aid Report (SAR): A form sent to the student after submitting the FAFSA to the federal processor. The

SAR shows the information processed and indicates Pell Grant eligibility.

Student ID Number: A multi-code that uniquely identifies each student. At some institutions, the social security number is used as the student ID number.

Study Abroad Program: A program that gives students the opportunity to pursue educational opportunities in another country. Normally, students are enrolled in classes while studying abroad, and credits are transferred back to their home institution. Students can typically find out about these programs in the International Education office, Study Abroad or Foreign Language Department.

Subsidized Loan: A loan awarded based on financial need. When students take out subsidized loans they are not charged any interest before they begin repayment or during deferment periods.

Syllabus: The document that a professor provides as a course outline. A syllabus will usually include assignments, due dates, test dates, grading procedures, and attendance policies and an overview of the course. It is usually provided on the first day of class.

Taxable Income: Income included on tax returns: salaries, wages, tips, interest, and dividends minus deductions and exemptions.

Teaching Assistant (TA): A graduate or undergraduate student with teaching responsibilities.

Traditional Student: Students who are the typical undergraduate college student, usually aged 17-23.

Transcript: An official copy of a student's academic record available through either the Records and Registration Office or Registrar's Office.

Transfer Credit: Credit that was earned at another college or university.

Tuition: The amount charged per semester credit hour for instruction at a college or university.

Verification: A process of review to determine the accuracy of the information on a student's financial assistance application.

Undeclared Major: The status for students who have not yet decided upon a major program. First-year students usually come in as undeclared majors.

Undergraduate: A college or university student who has not yet earned a bachelor's degree.

Unit: A specific measure of value ascribed to satisfactory completion a course of study; sometimes referred to as credits or hours.

University: An assembly of colleges, each specializing in a different field.

Unsubsidized Loan: A loan that is not granted based on need. Unsubsidized loans charge interest from the time the loan is awarded until the time it is paid in full. These loans have no grace period.

Withdraw: The process of voluntarily leaving a course or the university without academic penalty. A "W" letter grade will be placed on the student's transcript for each course attempted. Typically, once the class is repeated, the W letter grade will be replaced by the new letter grade.

Work-Study Programs: A program offered by many colleges and universities that allow students to work part time during the school year as part of their financial aid package. Students can usually apply for these jobs in the student employment office or financial aid office.

W-2: Statement used for income tax purposes. W-2 forms are sent to an employee and show gross earnings and deductions (such as federal, state, and local income taxes and FICA) for a calendar year. The W-2 Form is a necessary document for filing for financial aid as it can determine if a student is eligible for financial aid. It is also called a wage and tax statement.

Sophomore Student Resources
Useful Websites

Here are some websites and books that are helpful in your postsecondary education journey.

Accreditation:

http://www.chea.org/search/default.asp
Council for Higher Education Accreditation (CHEA) database

Athletic Scholarships:

www.edref.com/athletic-scholarships
www.ncaa.org/about/scholarships.html

Campus Safety:

www.collegesafe.com

Career Services Support Websites:

http://www.collegegrad.com
http://www.interbiznet.com/hunt
www.monster.com

Sophomore Success

College Research and Homework Websites:

http://www.algebra-online.com
Algebra Online
http://www.encyberpedia.com/ency.htm
Encyberpedia
www.bjpinchbeck.com
Homework Helper
http://www.libraryspot.com
Library Spot
http://www.loc.gov
Library of Congress
http://www.refdesk.com/main.html
My Virtual Reference Desk
http://www.s9.com/biography
Noble Citizens of Planet Earth
http://www.onelook.com
One Look Dictionaries
www.dictionary.com
Online Dictionary
http://owl.english.purdue.edu
Online Writing Lab-Purdue University
http://www.sci.lib.uci.edu/~martindale/Ref.html
Reference Desk
http://www.ipl.org/ref
Reference Center
http://www.researchpaper.com/directory.html
Researchpaper.com
http://www.studyweb.com
Study Web
http://thorplus.lib.purdue.edu/reference/index.html
The Virtual Reference Desk

Sophomore Success

College Search Information

http://www.collegeispossible.org
American Council on Education
http://www.aihec.org
American Indian Higher Education Consortium
http://www.community-college.org
Community College Directory
http://www.cccu.org/about/members.asp
Council for Christian Colleges and Universities
http://www.privatecolleges.com
Directory of Private Colleges and Universities
http://www.hacu.net/hacu
Hispanic Association of Colleges and Universities
Directory
http://www.ed.gov/about/inits/list/whhbcu/edlite-list.html
Historically Black College and University Directory
http://www.clas.ufl.edu/au
Index of American Universities
www.braintrack.com
The World's Most Complete Education-Index
http://www.campustours.com
Virtual Campus Tours

Financial Aid Information:

http://www.college-scholarships.com
http://www.collegeboundfund.com
http://www.edfund.org
htpp://www.educaid.com
http://www.fafsa.ed.gov
http://www.finaid.org

Sophomore Success

http://www.freegovmoney.net
http://www.nela.net
http://www.salliemae.com

General Scholarship Information

http://www.fastweb.com
http://www.freescholarshipsearch.com
http://scholarshipcoach.com
http://www.scholarshipexpert.com
http://www.scholarships.com
http://www.srnexpress.com

Health Information

http://www.nalusda.gov/fnic
Food and Nutrition Information
http://www.menshealth.com
Men's Health Daily
http://www.shapeup.org/sua
Shape Up America
http://www.womens-health.com
Women's Health Interactive

Learning Styles and Learning Disabilities

http://www.chadd.org
Children and Adults with Attention Deficit Disorder
http://www.keirsey.com
Keirsey Web Site

Sophomore Success

New/Used College Textbooks Online

www.abebooks.com
www.bigwords.com
www.bookfinder.com
www.bookmooch.com
www.cheapestbookprice.com
www.efollett.com
www.textbook411.com
www.textbooks.com
www.thriftbooks.com
www.valorebooks.com
www.varsitybooks.com

Resident Assistant and Higher Education Career Information

www.Academic360.com
http://www.acuho.ohio-state.edu
www.HigherEdJobs.com
www.residentassistant.com
www.resnet.com
www.studentaffairs.com

SAT and ACT Information

www.act.org
ACT Information
www.collegeboard.com
SAT and ACT Information

Sophomore Success

Study Abroad Information

http://www.iie.org//programs/gilman/index.html
Benjamin A. Gillman Scholarship
http://www.iie.org/pgms
Institute of International Education
http://www.iefa.org
International Education Financial Aid
http://www.internationalscholarships.com
International Scholarships Online
http://www.thescholarship.com
The Scholar Ship
http://www.semesteratsea.com
Semester at Sea
http://www.studyabroad.com
StudyAroad.com

ABOUT THE AUTHOR

Tawan Perry, M.Ed., is a nationally renowned student leadership expert and an award winning author. As an undergraduate student, he served as both SGA Vice President and as a resident assistant. After graduating from college, he worked at various institutions as a housing administrator, Greek advisor, and assistant dean.

Tawan is a leading authority on the sophomore experience in college and has been a featured guest on FOX, CBS, and NBC. He is the creator of the comprehensive **Connect-5 College Completion** program designed to help students graduate from college by providing support each year of college. He is the author of **8** books and a regular contributor to national magazines. Tawan currently resides in Raleigh, N.C.

For more information and to book Tawan for your events, visit http://tawanperry.com

More Products from Tawan Perry

College Sense: What College and High School Advisors Don't Tell You about College

Making sense of higher education can confound the most stellar of students. Your college education isn't just about gaining knowledge, but an experience unlike any other you will have in life. Navigating the college environment is about learning the language: If you know how the system works, you can understand and prepare for the complexities that college presents.

It explores a myriad of essential topics, such as how to reduce and eliminate debt, the questions that you should ask during your campus visit, and how to get the most of your college experience. It's the only book you'll ever need to help you prepare for all those things that your advisors didn't tell you about college. *College Sense* **was the 2008 National Best Books award winner for college guides.**

College Sense is ideal for:

☑ Any incoming first year student

☑ High school or PTA that want to give graduating seniors an invaluable gift

☑ Any community college student that will be transferring into a 4-year institution

☑ Non-profit organizations that want to give students an advantage in college

☑ University 101 college course textbook

College Sense for Parents

Each year college becomes gradually more expensive, and families find themselves desperately looking for ways to reduce rising costs. *College Sense for Parents* offers help by providing several time-tested strategies that will eliminate debt and reduce the cost of college. This audio recording covers topics such as how to reduce the cost of tuition, board, books, application fees, and other related college expenses. Listen to it on your way to work or in the comfort of your home. *College Sense for Parents* gets straight to the point and offers tips that will easily save you thousands of dollars. This is a **must have** for any parent with college bound children.

Quote These (College Edition)

Whether you are an incoming freshmen or a procrastinating senior, ***Quote These*** is the most astounding book of quotes ever assembled to assist and inspire college students. Categorized by such themes as transition, relationships and time management, this book is a great resource whether you're writing speeches, personal statements, essays, or just looking for guidance during those often riddle filled college years.

Students Go to College For Free: How to Get a B.S. without the B.S.

If you're stressed out about how to pay for your college education or looking for a way to get your degree without going into a lifetime of debt, *Students Go to College For Free* has the solution. A **must read** book for students at all levels, advisors and counselors too, this book shows you how to attend a tuition-free college, attend prestigious schools without the ACT or SAT, get your master's degree and doctorate for free, pay in-state tuition even if you're out of state, and how to earn 30 or more college credits before taking a college class.

Up Your Org: A Guide to Help Student Leaders Thrive

This hands-on guide is a blueprint of how to be a successful campus leader, packed with information and tools to equip you to become a great student leader, whatever your position is in the organization. Student leaders will discover: how to run more efficient and fun meetings that still get things done; how to get buy-in, even from apathetic students; effective ways to partner well with administration and other campus organizations; new ways to create a more inclusive and safer campus community; how to create dynamic programs that will be well attended even on a shoestring budget, and ways to re-energize your student organization in the best and worst of times.

Up Your Org: A Guide to Help Club Advisors Thrive

A GUIDE TO HELP
CLUB
ADVISORS
THRIVE
TAWAN PERRY

Whether you are a first-time advisor or a seasoned advisor, this guide will help you to better serve student leaders and create an enriching campus environment. Club advisors will discover: how to effortlessly transition student leaders from one year to the next; creative ways to motivate unenthusiastic student leaders; how to masterfully balance home and work life; how to market events that will result in standing room only attendance; how to organize a well-attended conference from start to finish; resourceful ideas that will help you uphold your budget; fun and affordable programming ideas, sample event calendars, and assessment forms.

Up Your Org: A Guide to Help Orientation Leaders Thrive

Whether you are a seasoned orientation leader or first-time, this guide will help you to better serve new students and create an enriching collegiate campus experience starting day one. Orientation leaders will discover: creative ways to connect students to your campus as soon as they arrive on campus; how to masterfully balance and prioritize the first eight weeks of the school year; how to market events that will result in standing room only attendance; how to organize a well-attended event from start to finish; fun and enjoyable ice breakers for all and practical event evaluation forms.

Editor

Cynthia Bull is an internationally published writer and editor who helps international authors, marketers and speakers add greater value to their products through her top-quality writing, editing and transcription services. She is the author of *How To Be A Medical Transcriptionist* and *Winning At Work While Balancing Your Life,* a contributing author of *Walking with the Wise Entrepreneur* (Mentors Publishing House), cited in *Make BIG Profits on eBay* (Entrepreneur Press), and Managing Editor of *Mentors Magazine Think & Grow Rich Edition.*

Cynthia has created over 400 book products in recent years for her clients, and as mentor helps clients reach their goals through her products, experience, and genuine caring. She has been a contributing writer for an online organization dedicated to helping small businesses succeed. For more information she can be contacted at:

www.cynrje.com
www.cynrjetranscription.com

Made in the USA
Coppell, TX
19 March 2022

75223938R00069